BAAL KADMO[N]

Calling Upon The God of New Beginnings

GANESHA MANTRA MAGICK

Ganesha Mantra Magick

Calling Upon The God Of New Beginnings

Copyright information

Copyright © 2016 by Baal Kadmon

All rights reserved. No part of this book may be reproduced by any mechanical, photographic, or electrical process, or in the form of a recording. Nor may it be stored in a storage/retrieval system nor transmitted or otherwise be copied for private or public use-other than "fair use" as quotations in articles or reviews—without the prior written consent of the Author. The Information in this book is solely for educational purposes and not for the treatment, diagnosis or prescription of any diseases. This text is not meant to provide financial or health advice of any sort. The Author and the publisher are in no way liable for any use or misuse of the material. No Guarantee of results are being made in this text.

Kadmon, Baal

Ganesha Mantra Magick – **Calling Upon The God Of New Beginnings**

–1st ed

Printed in the United States of America

Cover image : #119535132

Hand drawn elephant head tribal style. Hindu Lord Ganesha vector © J_kaBook Cover Design: Baal Kadmon

At the best of our ability we have credited those who created the pictures based on the research we have conducted. If there are images in the book that have not been given due copyright notice please contact us at Resheph@baalkadmon.com and we will remedy the situation by giving proper copyright credit or we will remove the image/s at your request.

Disclaimer

Disclaimer: By law, I need to add this statement.

This book is for educational purposes only and does not claim to prevent or cure any disease. The advice and methods in this book should not be construed as financial, medical or psychological treatment. Please seek advice from a professional if you have serious financial, medical or psychological issues.

By purchasing, reading and or listening to this book, you understand that results are not guaranteed. In light of this, you understand that in the event that this book or audio does not work or causes harm in any area of your life, you agree that you do not hold Baal Kadmon, Amazon, its employees or affiliates liable for any damages you may experience or incur.

The Text and or Audio in this series are copyrighted 2016.

The God of New Beginnings

Ganesha also known more commonly in the west as Ganesh, is one of the most beloved, if not the most beloved deity in Hinduism. He is best known for his ability to help people remove obstacles in their lives. Although this Is my first book on Ganesh, I have taught people the Ganesh mantras and they have used it with great success. I have received several emails stating that the Ganesh mantra added that extra spark they needed in their lives. Not only did it take their mantra work to a new level, some also used it in conjunction with western magick and he came through for them.

Ganesh has an elephant head and this fact makes him very easy to recognize. However, what he is most known for his willingness and ability to help people remove obstacles in their lives. In addition to that, he is also a patron of the arts and sciences and has been known to help people with these fields as well. He is so effective that his worship can be found outside of Hinduism as well. Jains and Buddhists are also known to have devotion towards him.

Although I do not have a main practice to Ganesh, I have used his power several times and can attest to his efficacy as can so many people, not only in my sphere, but the millions around the world.

In this book, we will be tapping into his power for the following purposes:

To Remove Obstacles (general).

To Gain Financial Prosperity. Can Be used For Good Health As well.

To Gain Extreme Good Luck In All Endeavors

To Help You in All Your Relationships, Including Romantic ones.

To Help You Remove Stress in Your Life.

To Gain Leadership Skills

To Quiet Ones Ego

To Achieve Spiritual Unity with the Divine

Here is an example of one of His most popular Mantras: Like most of the Gods and Goddesses, there are several Mantras for each deity. This one, however, is the most popular. It is in many ways a "catch-all."

The Mantra:

Om Gam Ganapataye Namah

Loosely Defined as 'Salutations To Ganesha the remover of obstacles.'

Pronounced: OM GUM GUNA-PA-TA-YEY NA-MA-HA

We will discuss some of his many mantras later in this book. Now let us now cover some of his history.

If you feel you need help with Mantra pronunciations, I have Audios you may find useful. Please go to:

www.baalkadmon.com/mantra-audio-marketplace/

The Most Beloved Of The Gods

Ganesh is by far the most recognized of all the Hindu God. He is the only one with the head of an elephant. Every occultist I know that works with Sanskrit mantras and Hindu magick love working with him. Even my friends who are firmly on the left-hand path and tend to work only with demonic entities, will find themselves working with him as well. He, in many ways, is a gentle energy that helps buffer some of the more intense left hand energies. Since he is predominantly a god of the right hand, our work with him will reflect this.

In India, many know him not as Ganesha but as Ganapati, thus the **"Ganapataye"** in his main mantra that we recited in the previous chapter. He is not only the remover of obstacles but he is also the God of Learning, the arts and of wisdom. As I called him in the previous chapter, he is the God of New beginnings and it is for this reason they invoke him upon new ventures.

Many people may not know this but Ganesha is often known to be the one who wrote the entire Hindu epic, the Mahabharata from the dictation of Vyasa. Another claim to fame for Ganesh is that he is the son of Shiva and Parvati, who I cover in my book "Shiva Mantra Magick."

Ganesh is truly a loving and warm energy and I am very eager to teach you his main mantras. However, as I am want to do in all my books, I would like to give more background information on this wonderful God.

Ganesha's Story

As stated in the previous chapter, Ganesh is the son of Shiva and Parvati. One would wonder with such beautiful parents, how did he gain his Elephant headed form?

As the story goes, Parvati formed Ganesh without Shivas cooperation. She shaped him into the likeness of a youth. At first, Shiva thought that Parvati betrayed him so he struck of the head of the boy. When he realized the stupendous error he has made, he tried to heal the lad. Unfortunately, the head of the boy was washed away in the Ganges and was subsequently consumed by fish. Shiva solved this by having the head of the first creature seen to be cut off and placed atop the decapitated boy. And of course, the first living creature seen was the elephant. It is ONE reason Ganesha will forever be associated with the elephant. There are other stories as well. In some, he is not formed by Parvati but is, in fact, born of Shiva and Parvati, other stories say he was simply discovered by Shiva and Parvati and that he is not their son. Another story suggests that he is the son of the elephant headed Goddess Malini after she drank Parvati's bath water. So as you can see, a few stories exist.

In the most common representations of Ganesh, he appears as a pot-bellied figure as well. In his four hands, he holds a shell, a discus, a club, and a water lily. Like most of the Hindu Gods, he rides a top an animal, in his case a rat. The rat is not just a normal rat, he is, in fact a giant Ganesh defeated and in his defeat, he metamorphosed into a rat. Ganesh, although very kind and benign is not a weak God. He is in fact very powerful and is often employed in the various wars the Gods have partaken in throughout the millennia.

In many hindu books, a prayer to Ganesh is present. His image is found on doors and statues of him exist on many altars throughout India. **Suffice it to say, he is a God we want on our side.**

His Divine Family

Aside from his divine parentage, his divine family also contains brothers. His brother is the God of war and is known by a few different names. The most popular one is Kartikeya, that is the name I too learned when studying Hinduism. He is also known as Murugan or Skanda. It is not exactly clear if Ganesh is considered the eldest since in different regions of India, the birth order changes. In north India, Ganesha is the youngest of the two; while in the south, Ganesha is the older of the two. Although we know Ganesh to be the more popular from the divine sons, it was not always so. From 500 BC to 600 AD Skanda was much more popular.

We are not sure if Ganesh has a consort. He may be single ladies. However, he has attributes such as Buddhi or Intellectual power, Siddhi or spiritual power and Riddhi the power of prosperity. These attributes are considered mostly feminine in nature so in many ways he may be a male God but his inner energy is very infused with Shakti. Some say those are not, in fact, attributes but names of Goddesses or Ganesha wives. The texts do not make this clear. It is understood that Ganesh has 2 sons but it is not always clear what their names are. It changes based on the region of India. In the next chapter, we will discuss Ganesha as he appears in certain Hindu Texts.

Hindu Texts That Mention Ganesh

During part of the Puranic period, mainly 600-1330 AD Ganesha starts to appear in the literature more prominently. It is here where we find the early stories of Ganesha such as his birth, parenthood and how he obtained an elephants head. Unlike some of the other Gods, he is nowhere to be found in the Vedic tradition. In the 9th century his cult status started to really grow and was considered one of the primary deities. The other deities that came to prominence during this time were Shiva, Vishnu, Devi and Surya. I will not go into them right now, but perhaps in a future release.

The Puranas that mention him specifically are the Mudgala Purana, Ganesha Puranas , the Ganapati Atharvashirsa Purana and the Ganesha Sahasranama which is considered part of the Puranic class of documents. In these Puranas a specific Ganesha practice was formed call the " Ganapatya" tradition. He does not really appear that much in other texts of weighty spiritual significance.

In the next chapter, we will go through his mantras quickly and after that we will get to the ritual portion of the book.

Ganesh Mantras

In this book we will cover 8 Mantras specifically to Ganesh and his various names he is known to have. Mantras in and of themselves are very powerful and should always be used with respect and with your full attention. I created this book in such a way that it will be easy for you to maintain focus on the mantras. In this chapter I will just go over them and then in the next chapter we will use them in rituals.

To Remove Obstacles (general).

To Gain Financial Prosperity. Can Be used For Good Health As well.

To Gain Extreme Good Luck In All Endeavors

To Help You in All Your Relationships, Including Romantic ones.

To Help You Remove Stress in Your Life.

To Gain Leadership Skills

To Quiet Ones Ego

To Achieve Spiritual Unity with the Divine

MANTRA 1

Om Gam Ganapataye Namah

Pronounced: OM GUM GUNA-PA-TA-YEY NA-MA-HA

This Mantra is his general mantra that is in many ways a catch all. In this book we will use it for a general removal of Obstacles

MANTRA 2

OM HREENG GREENG HREENG

Pronounced: 'OM HREENG GREENG HREENG

This mantra is used To Gain Financial Prosperity. Can Be used For Good Health As well.

MANTRA 3

VAKRA-TUNNDDA MAHA-KAAYA SURYA-KOTTI SAMAPRABHA
NIRVIGHNAM KURU ME DEVA SARVA-KAARYESHU SARVADAA

Pronounced: 'VAKRA TOON-DA MAHA-KA-YA SURYA-KOTEE SAMA-PRAB-HA NEER-VIG-NAM KURU ME DEVA SARVA KA-AR-YESHU SAR-VA-DA

This mantra is used to To Gain Extreme Good Luck In All Endeavors

MANTRA 4

OM VIGNANAASHNAY NAMAH

Pronounced: 'OM VIGNA-NA-ASH-NAY NAMA

This mantra is used To Help You in All Your Relationships, Including Romantic ones.

MANTRA 5

OM GAJKARNIKAYA NAMAH

Pronounced: 'OM GAJ-CAR-NEE-KAYA NA-MA'

This mantra is used to remove stress from your life.

MANTRA 6

OM GANADHYAKSHAYA NAMAH

Pronounced: 'OM GANA-DEE-YAK-SHA-YA NA-MA'

This mantra is used to gain leadership skills.

MANTRA 7

OM GAJANANAYA NAMAH

Pronounced: 'OM GAJAN-AN-NAYA NA-MA

This mantra is used to quiet the ego.

MANTRA 8

OM LAMBODARAYA NAMAH

Pronounced: 'OM LAMBO-DA-RAYA NA-MA'

This mantra is used To Achieve Spiritual Unity with the Divine

What You Will Need For Ganesh Rituals

Before we proceed, here is a list of thing you can use to enhance your magick **(IF YOU DO NOT HAVE THESE ITEMS IT IS PERFECTLY OKAY, THEY SIMPLY ENHANCE YOUR RITUAL)**

1. A "picture" or statue if Ganesh. I have this one: [Rare Lord Ganesh Ganesha Beautiful Statues Hindu Good Luck God - White Statues](#)
2. Candy, any kind will do, Ganesh is known for his love of candy and we will use it as an offering.
3. The following Incense: [Shree Ganesh - Box of Six 20 Stick Tubes, 120 Sticks Total - HEM Incense](#)
4. (Any incense will do, I just prefer this one)
5. The following Candles: [Red Chime Candles](#) [Gold Candles](#) [White Candles](#) [Silver candles](#) [Blue Candles](#) [Black Candles](#)
6. A secure plate or candle holder to hold the candles. Since the ones I recommend vary in size you can use any make or brand of your choosing. Just make sure to find one that will hold these candles and will allow for safety (NEVER LEAVE CANDLES BURNING UNATTENDED)

7. An Incense holder. (NEVER LEAVE INCENSE BURNING UNATTENDED)
8. TIBETAN BUDDHIST MEDITATION 108 BEADS

Let me now explain the rationale behind the objects above.

1. The Statue and the candy: This is to focus your attention. I find it helps me "feel" The god's presence when I do a ritual to him. The candy is an offering.

2. The Incense: This Incense is a wonderful sacred fragrance.

3. **Candles: (Please note you can buy any kind of candle you like, they don't have to be chimes or votive. I just happen to like the ones I provided here)**

Red Chime Candles: This color is quite powerful

Gold Candles: This candle will be used for the ritual on financial assistance. Many occultists will tell you to use green, but this has been a long-held misconception. The only reason why people have said to use green is because it's the color of money. The thing is, it's only the color of money in the USA and maybe a few notes here and there of other nations. They don't call the dollar "greenback" for nothing. Green is not a color that is truly indicative money. Gold is though, Gold is UNIVERSALLY known to be a signifier of wealth both in ancient times and present. If you have been using Green for your money rituals, now you know to use gold instead. It is much more effective.

White Candles: White is for purity

Silver candles: This is the color of wisdom as well as for magickal powers.

Blue Candles: This will be used for health

Black Candles: These candles will be used to conquer your ego

TIBETAN BUDDHIST MEDITATION 108 BEADS: These beads are very helpful for keeping track of your mantra recitations.

In the following Chapters, we will go through all 8 rituals. Each ritual will have its own chapter.

Introduction To The Rituals

Below you will find 8 rituals, very simple but powerful ones. Each ritual can be done at any time.

Here are the rituals we will be performing:

- To Remove Obstacles (general).
- To Gain Financial Prosperity. Can Be used For Good Health As well.
- To Gain Extreme Good Luck In All Endeavors
- To Help You in All Your Relationships, Including Romantic ones.
- To Help You Remove Stress in Your Life.
- To Gain Leadership Skills
- To Quiet Ones Ego
- To Achieve Spiritual Unity with the Divine

I will walk you through each ritual step by step... Let us now call upon Ganesh the remover of obstacles.

If you feel you need help with Mantra pronunciations, I have Audios you may find useful. Please go to:

www.baalkadmon.com/mantra-audio-marketplace/

To Remove Obstacles

Please setup a place in your abode that you can dedicate to this ritual. If you have an altar, that is superb but if you don't, any place in your home where the ritual can be performed is good too.

1. Place the picture or statue of Ganesh at the Center.

2. To the left of the image, place the white candle and light it.

3. In the back or to the right, please light the incense.

4. Place some candy at Ganeshs feet as an offering

5. Sit quietly and Think about the obstacles you need removed.

6. Say the Ganesh Mantra 108 times.

Om Gam Ganapataye Namah

Pronounced: OM GUM GUNA-PA-TA-YEY NA-MA-HA

7. Now look at the image or statue intently and feel his presence resonate with you. You may notice that the

image takes up your entire visual field. Sit with that for as long as you wish.

8. When you are satisfied, you may let the candles and incense burn to completion. (Please be sure not to leave them unattended. If you need to leave your abode, you may extinguish them and ignite them upon your return.)

Thus concludes this ritual. You may leave the statue on the altar or put it away. You may offer the candy to nature OR better yet, consume some or all of it yourself and enjoy it.

You will not need to do this ritual again. HOWEVER, I do suggest you recite this mantra at least 108 times every day for 40 days after performing the initial ritual or until you get what you desire.

I have created a mantra audio for this mantra. Please go to http://baalkadmon.com/product/ganesh-mantras

To Gain Financial Prosperity

Please setup a place in your abode that you can dedicate to this ritual. If you have an altar, that is superb but if you don't, any place in your home where the ritual can be performed is good too.

1. Place the picture or statue of Ganesh at the Center.

2. To the left of the image, place the Gold candle and light it.

3. In the back or to the right, please light the incense.

4. Place some candy at Ganeshs feet as an offering

5. Sit quietly and Think about the financial prosperity that you need. It can be anything.

6. Say the Ganesh Mantra 108 times.

OM HREENG GREENG HREENG

Pronounced: 'OM HREENG GREENG HREENG

7. Now look at the image or statue intently and feel his presence resonate with you. You may notice that the image takes up your entire visual field. Sit with that for as long as you wish.

8. When you are satisfied, you may let the candles and incense burn to completion. (Please be sure not to leave them unattended. If you need to leave your abode, you may extinguish them and ignite them upon your return.)

Thus concludes this ritual. You may leave the statue on the altar or put it away. You may offer the candy to nature OR better yet, consume some or all of it yourself and enjoy it.

You will not need to do this ritual again. HOWEVER, I do suggest you recite this mantra at least 108 times every day for 40 days after performing the initial ritual or until you get what you desire.

I have created a mantra audio for this mantra. Please go to http://baalkadmon.com/product/ganesh-mantras

To Gain Extreme Good Luck

Please setup a place in your abode that you can dedicate to this ritual. If you have an altar, that is superb but if you don't, any place in your home where the ritual can be performed is good too.

1. Place the picture or statue of Ganesh at the Center.

2. To the left of the image, place the gold candle and light it.

3. In the back or to the right, please light the incense.

4. Place some candy at Ganeshs feet as an offering

5. Sit quietly and think about what good luck means to you. Is it for something specific? Or general?

6. Say the Ganesh Mantra 108 times.

**VAKRA-TUNNDDA MAHA-KAAYA SURYA-KOTTI SAMAPRABHA
NIRVIGHNAM KURU ME DEVA SARVA-KAARYESHU SARVADAA**

Pronounced: 'VAKRA TOON-DA MAHA-KA-YA SURYA-KOTEE SAMA-PRAB-HA NEER-VIG-NAM KURU ME DEVA SARVA KA-AR-YESHU SAR-VA-DA

7. Now look at the image or statue intently and feel his presence resonate with you. You may notice that the image takes up your entire visual field. Sit with that for as long as you wish.

8. When you are satisfied, you may let the candles and incense burn to completion. (Please be sure not to leave them unattended. If you need to leave your abode, you may extinguish them and ignite them upon your return.)

Thus concludes this ritual. You may leave the statue on the altar or put it away. You may offer the candy to nature OR better yet, consume some or all of it yourself and enjoy it.

You will not need to do this ritual again. HOWEVER, I do suggest you recite this mantra at least 108 times every day for 40 days after performing the initial ritual or until you get what you desire.

I have created a mantra audio for this mantra. Please go to http://baalkadmon.com/product/ganesh-mantras

To Help You In All Relationships

Please setup a place in your abode that you can dedicate to this ritual. If you have an altar, that is superb but if you don't, any place in your home where the ritual can be performed is good too.

1. Place the picture or statue of Ganesh at the Center.

2. To the left of the image, place the red candle and light it.

3. In the back or to the right, please light the incense.

4. Place some candy at Ganeshs feet as an offering

5. Sit quietly and think about the relationship you need fixing Or improving.

6. Say the Ganesh Mantra 108 times.

OM VIGNANAASHNAY NAMAH

Pronounced: 'OM VIGNA-NA-ASH-NAY NAMA

7. Now look at the image or statue intently and feel his presence resonate with you. You may notice that the image takes up your entire visual field. Sit with that for as long as you wish.

8. When you are satisfied, you may let the candles and incense burn to completion. (Please be sure not to leave them unattended. If you need to leave your abode, you may extinguish them and ignite them upon your return.)

Thus concludes this ritual. You may leave the statue on the altar or put it away. You may offer the candy to nature OR better yet, consume some or all of it yourself and enjoy it.

You will not need to do this ritual again. HOWEVER, I do suggest you recite this mantra at least 108 times every day for 40 days after performing the initial ritual or until you get what you desire.

I have created a mantra audio for this mantra. Please go to http://baalkadmon.com/product/ganesh-mantras

To Help You Remove Stress

Please setup a place in your abode that you can dedicate to this ritual. If you have an altar, that is superb but if you don't, any place in your home where the ritual can be performed is good too.

1. Place the picture or statue of Ganesh at the Center.

2. To the left of the image, place the blue candle and light them.

3. In the back or to the right, please light the incense.

4. Place some candy at Ganeshs feet as an offering

5. Sit quietly and think about what is causing you stress and your intention to rid yourself of it

6. Say the Ganesh Mantra 108 times.

OM GAJKARNIKAYA NAMAH

Pronounced: 'OM GAJ-CAR-NEE-KAYA NA-MA'

7. Now look at the image or statue intently and feel his presence resonate with you. You may notice that the image takes up your entire visual field. Sit with that for as long as you wish.

8. When you are satisfied, you may let the candles and incense burn to completion. (Please be sure not to leave them unattended. If you need to leave your abode, you may extinguish them and ignite them upon your return.)

Thus concludes this ritual. You may leave the statue on the altar or put it away. You may offer the candy to nature OR better yet, consume some or all of it yourself and enjoy it.

You will not need to do this ritual again. HOWEVER, I do suggest you recite this mantra at least 108 times every day for 40 days after performing the initial ritual or until you get what you desire.

I have created a mantra audio for this mantra. Please go to http://baalkadmon.com/product/ganesh-mantras

To Gain Leadership Skills

Please setup a place in your abode that you can dedicate to this ritual. If you have an altar, that is superb but if you don't, any place in your home where the ritual can be performed is good too.

1. Place the picture or statue of Ganesh at the Center.

2. To the left of the image, place the black candle and light it.

3. In the back or to the right, please light the incense.

4. Place some candy at Ganeshs feet as an offering

5. Sit quietly and think about your desire for leadership skills. Perhaps it is for a new job or on a project etc.

6. Say the Ganesh Mantra 108 times.

OM GANADHYAKSHAYA NAMAH

Pronounced: 'OM GANA-DEE-YAK-SHA-YA NA-MA'

7. Now look at the image or statue intently and feel his presence resonate with you. You may notice that the image takes up your entire visual field. Sit with that for as long as you wish.

8. When you are satisfied, you may let the candles and incense burn to completion. (Please be sure not to leave them unattended. If you need to leave your abode, you may extinguish them and ignite them upon your return.)

Thus concludes this ritual. You may leave the statue on the altar or put it away. You may offer the candy to nature OR better yet, consume some or all of it yourself and enjoy it.

You will not need to do this ritual again. HOWEVER, I do suggest you recite this mantra at least 108 times every day for 40 days after performing the initial ritual or until you get what you desire.

I have created a mantra audio for this mantra. Please go to http://baalkadmon.com/product/ganesh-mantras

To Quiet Ones Ego

Please setup a place in your abode that you can dedicate to this ritual. If you have an altar, that is superb but if you don't, any place in your home where the ritual can be performed is good too.

1. Place the picture or statue of Ganesh at the Center.

2. To the left of the image, place the white candle and light it.

3. In the back or to the right, please light the incense.

4. Place some candy at Ganeshs feet as an offering

5. Sit quietly and think about your desire to be rid of the interference of your ego. Is it harming you?

6. Say the Ganesh Mantra 108 times.

OM GAJANANAYA NAMAH

Pronounced: 'OM GAJAN-AN-NAYA NA-MA

7. Now look at the image or statue intently and feel his presence resonate with you. You may notice that the image takes up your entire visual field. Sit with that for as long as you wish.

8. When you are satisfied, you may let the candles and incense burn to completion. (Please be sure not to leave them unattended. If you need to leave your abode, you may extinguish them and ignite them upon your return.)

Thus concludes this ritual. You may leave the statue on the altar or put it away. You may offer the candy to nature OR better yet, consume some or all of it yourself and enjoy it.

You will not need to do this ritual again. HOWEVER, I do suggest you recite this mantra at least 108 times every day for 40 days after performing the initial ritual or until you get what you desire.

I have created a mantra audio for this mantra. Please go to http://baalkadmon.com/product/ganesh-mantras

To Achieve Spiritual Unity With the Divine

Please setup a place in your abode that you can dedicate to this ritual. If you have an altar, that is superb but if you don't, any place in your home where the ritual can be performed is good too.

1. Place the picture or statue of Ganesh at the Center.

2. To the left of the image, place the silver candle and light it.

3. In the back or to the right, please light the incense.

4. Place some candy at Ganeshs feet as an offering

5. Sit quietly and think about your desire to acquire unity consciousness with the divine. Think about what this means for you.

6. Say the Ganesh Mantra 108 times.

OM LAMBODARAYA NAMAH

Pronounced: 'OM LAMBO-DA-RAYA NA-MA'

7. Now look at the image or statue intently and feel his presence resonate with you. You may notice that the image takes up your entire visual field. Sit with that for as long as you wish.

8. When you are satisfied, you may let the candles and incense burn to completion. (Please be sure not to leave them unattended. If you need to leave your abode, you may extinguish them and ignite them upon your return.)

Thus concludes this ritual. You may leave the statue on the altar or put it away. You may offer the candy to nature OR better yet, consume some or all of it yourself and enjoy it.

You will not need to do this ritual again. HOWEVER, I do suggest you recite this mantra at least 108 times every day for 40 days after performing the initial ritual or until you get what you desire.

I have created a mantra audio for this mantra. Please go to http://baalkadmon.com/product/ganesh-mantras

How to Enhance Your Ganesh Mantra Practice - Achieving Siddhi

(Excerpted from Vashikaran Magick) Now that you have learned the mantras, I want to add some additional information here that will really up the effectiveness of these mantras and any mantra practice for that matter. As you saw, most of the mantras can be recited a few times and some, many more times. When doing so, you compound the energy upon itself and then it produces results. Its like a charge builds up and eventually fires, producing the goal. This is generally how mantras work and often once the result is achieved, the energy dissipates and that will be the end of the ritual. But what if you could ALWAYS embody the energy of the mantra? There is a way and It is called Siddhi.

Siddhi, in Sanskrit means "perfection" "accomplishment" and "Attainment" of magical abilities. When one achieves Siddhi with a particular mantra they acquire the actual energy of that mantra. So for example, the Main Attraction Seed Mantra is "Kleem". If you recite this 10,000 times in one sitting, you will have mastered the energy of this mantra and your attraction abilities will be enhanced and things will come naturally to you. After you achieve Siddhi, you will be unstoppable, with every recitation of the mantra after Siddhi you are a true and effective magician. Some schools of thought say that you do not need to do all 10,000 in one sitting but over 40 days. Follow your intuition on whether you want to do these chants in one sitting or several.

In saying this, if you want to enhance any of these mantras, I suggest chanting them 1,000 to 10,000 times in one sitting. I know this sounds like a lot, but once you get into the groove with the mantra the recitation will move very quickly. To keep track of this, I suggest you use Mala beads. I personally use this brand: TIBETAN BUDDHIST MEDITATION 108 BEADS

It has 108 beads; 108 is a sacred number and common in Hindu chanting. Although some of the mantras in this book require fewer than 108 recitation; I highly suggest you chant a mantra at least 108 times a day. With these Mala Beads, it will be easy to keep track. If you do 10 rounds of 108 recitations, you will be on your way to achieving Siddhi. You can, of course use any mala beads or create your own.

A Note On Mantra Pronunciation

As with most of my mantra magick titles, I have MP3 audios you can purchase if you are interested in learning how to pronounce the mantras in this book. The mantra Audio accompaniment for this book has each of the mantras in this book recited 108 times. These audios are often helpful, but are not a requirement.

If you feel you need help with Mantra pronunciations, I have Audios you may find useful. Please go to:

www.baalkadmon.com/mantra-audio-marketplace/

Conclusion

What you have learned here is VERY powerful and I suggest you use Ganesh whenever you feel you need help in your endeavors, it doesn't matter what they are. These mantras are like electricity, the energy will flow in the direction of the intended output. In saying that please be firm in your intentions and make sure what you want is truly what you want.

As they say, be careful what you ask for, you just might get it.

Other Books By The Author

Organized by date of publication from most recent:

Rabbi Isaac Luria: The Lion of the Kabbalah (Jewish Mystics Book 1)

Circe's Wand: Empowerment | Enchantment | Magick

Ganesha Mantra Magick: Calling Upon The God of New Beginnings

Shiva Mantra Magick: Harnessing The Primordial

Tefillin Magick: Using Tefillin For Magickal Purposes (Jewish Magick Book 1)

Jesus Magick (Bible Magick Book 2)

The Magickal Moment Of Now: The Inner Mind of the Advanced Magician

The Magick Of Lilith: Calling Upon The Great Goddess of The Left Hand Path (Mesopotamian Magick Book 1)

The Magickal Talismans of King Solomon

Mahavidya Mantra Magick: Tap Into the 10 Goddesses of Power

Jinn Magick: How to Bind the Jinn to do Your Bidding

Magick And The Bible: Is Magick Compatible With The Bible? (Bible Magick Book 1)

The Magickal Rites of Prosperity: Using Different Methods To Magickally Manifest Wealth

Lakshmi Mantra Magick: Tap Into The Goddess Lakshmi for Wealth and Abundance In All Areas of Life

Tarot Magick: Harness the Magickal Power of the Tarot

The Quantum Magician: Enhancing Your Magick With A Parallel Life

Tibetan Mantra Magick: Tap Into The Power Of Tibetan Mantras

The 42 Letter Name of God: The Mystical Name Of Manifestation (Sacred Names Book 6)

Tara Mantra Magick: How To Use The Power Of The Goddess Tara

Vedic Magick: Using Ancient Vedic Spells To Attain Wealth

The Daemonic Companion: Creating Daemonic Entities To Do Your Will

[Tap Into The Power Of The Chant: Attaining Supernatural Abilities Using Mantras (Supernatural Attainments Series](#)

[72 Demons Of The Name: Calling Upon The Great Demons Of The Name (Sacred Names Book 5)](#)

[Moldavite Magick: Tap Into The Stone Of Transformation Using Mantras (Crystal Mantra Magick Book 1)](#)

[Ouija Board Magick - Archangels Edition: Communicate And Harness The Power Of The Great Archangels](#)

[Chakra Mantra Magick: Tap Into The Magick Of Your Chakras (Mantra Magick Series Book 4)](#)

[Seed Mantra Magick: Master The Primordial Sounds Of The Universe (Mantra Magick Series Book 3)](#)

[The Magick Of Saint Expedite: Tap Into The Truly Miraculous Power Of Saint Expedite (Magick Of The Saints Book 2)](#)

[Kali Mantra Magick: Summoning The Dark Powers of Kali Ma (Mantra Magick Series Book 2)](#)

[Mary Magick: Calling Forth The Divine Mother For Help (Magick Of The Saints Book 1)](#)

Vashikaran Magick: Learn The Dark Mantras Of Subjugation (Mantra Magick Series Book 1)

The Hidden Names Of Genesis: Tap Into The Hidden Power Of Manifestation (Sacred Names Book 4)

The 99 Names Of Allah: Acquiring the 99 Divine Qualities of God (Sacred Names Book 3)

The 72 Angels Of The Name: Calling On the 72 Angels of God (Sacred Names)

The 72 Names of God: The 72 Keys To Transformation (Sacred Names Book 1)

About Author

Baal first discovered his occult gifts when he was very young. It was only in his teens when on a trip to the Middle East that he felt compelled to learn about what has been haunting him since childhood. Several teachers and many decades later he felt read to share what he has learned.

His teaching are unconventional to say the least. He shatters the beloved and idolatrously held notions most occultists hold dear. His pared-down approach to magick is a refreshing and is much-needed in a field that is mired by self-important magicians who place more important on pomp and circumstance rather than on magick. What you learn from Baal is straight forward with no frills. Magick is about bringing about change or a desired result, Magick is a natural birthright...There is no need to complicate it. Don't you agree?

If you have any questions please feel free to visit Baal at

http://www.BAALKADMON.COM

http://facebook.com/baal.kadmon

Printed in Great Britain
by Amazon